NEW YEAR'S BABY
WRITTEN BY AMELIA MEDEL

CELEBRATING THE JOY AND EXCITEMENT OF NEW YEAR'S

ISBN: 9798866684892

NEW YEAR'S IS AN EXCITING TIME

NEW YEAR'S DAY,
WE PREPARE

FOR THE PARTY,
WE BAKE FRESH COOKIES

I WRITE MY NEW YEAR'S RESOLUTIONS

WE POP
CHRISTMAS CRACKERS
AND WEAR A PAPER CROWN

GRANDMA WEARS
A FANCY GOWN

MOMMY HIDES GOLD COINS
IN FRESH WARM CAKES

ONE FULL OF LOVE,
AND NOT MUCH STRIFE

ABOUT THE AUTHOR

AMELIA MEDEL IS A PEDIATRIC OCCUPATIONAL THERAPIST. INSPIRED BY THE HOLIDAYS, AMELIA WROTE 'NEW YEAR'S BABY' TO HIGHLIGHT THE JOYS AND WONDER OF THE HOLIDAY SEASON.

AMELIA HAS WRITTEN SEVERAL OTHER BOOKS INCLUDING 'CHRISTMAS BABY' AND 'VALENTINE'S BABY'

27097117R00019